Creatures of the Dark

CONTENTS

A World of Darkness 2

Seeing in the Dark 4

Sounds in the Dark 8

Flying Blind 10

Safety in the Dark 12

Escaping the Heat 14

Caves and Burrows 16

Underwater Darkness 18

In the Garden 20

Catching a Glimpse 22

Glossary and Index 24

A World of Darkness

At the end of each day, when darkness falls, many creatures are just waking up. These creatures are *nocturnal* animals. They are active at night, and they sleep during the day.

Tawny frogmouths

Other creatures live in places that are dark all the time, such as deep caves, or the bottom of the ocean.

Seeing in the Dark

Eyes need light to work. Humans can see well when there is plenty of light. But many nocturnal animals can see well when there is very little light.

Many nocturnal animals, like this mouse lemur, have very large eyes.

The eyes of some nocturnal animals, like this palm civet, seem to shine at night. This is because some of the light they receive is reflected out again.

Many nocturnal animals have a kind of mirror in their eyes, known as a *tapetum*. The tapetum reflects the light that the eyes receive; this makes the light seem stronger and helps the animal to see.

Some animals that are active at night also come out in the daytime. Their eyes need to be able to adjust to different amounts of light.

The pupil (the dark central part of the eye) lets in the light. Cats' pupils become narrow slits in daylight. In the dark, they open wide to let in as much light as possible.

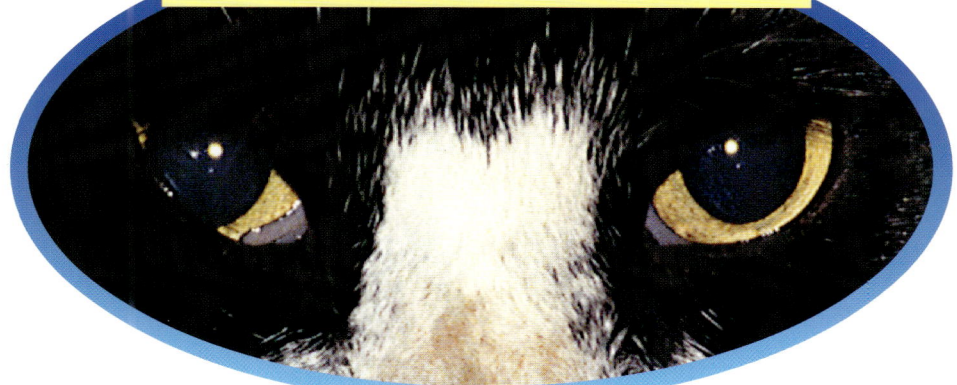

Sounds in the Dark

In the dark, many creatures rely on their sense of hearing to help them move around safely. Many nocturnal animals can hear very faint sounds – even a leaf falling.

Large ears help the fennec fox to hear faint, night sounds.

Barn owls use hearing as well as sight to find their food.

Flying Blind

Bats are almost completely blind. They use sounds to find their way and to hunt for their food.

Bats make very *high-pitched* sounds – too high for people to hear. These sounds bounce off objects and produce echoes. A bat can tell where an object is by listening to the echo that travels back. This process is called *echolocation*.

Bats sleep during the day, hanging upside down in trees or caves.

Safety in the Dark

For many creatures, the dark night is the safest time to be out and about.

Some flightless birds, such as kiwis, spend the day in burrows and come out at night to look for food.

Kiwis have an excellent sense of smell. Their long, flexible beaks have nostrils at the end, which help them to sniff out worms and insects.

Elephant hawk moth

Some moths are nocturnal. They rest during the day, hiding from hunters such as spiders and birds. At night they go in search of flowers and their nectar.

But the night is not completely safe. Moths must always be listening for bats. When moths sense bats approaching, they stop flying and drop straight to the ground.

Escaping the Heat

Deserts can be burning hot during the day. Some desert animals avoid the hot sun by coming out only at night.

Grasshopper mice come out of their burrows at night. They howl outside the burrow to scare other animals.

At night, deserts can be very cold. Many nocturnal animals, such as sandcats, have thick coats to keep them warm.

Gerbils come out at night to collect water from seeds covered with dew.

Caves and Burrows

Some creatures live in darkness all the time.

Moles spend their lives in dark tunnels. They are almost completely blind, and depend on the senses of touch and smell.

A mole's nostrils are on the side of its snout. This stops them from filling up with dirt and mud.

Glowworms produce a faint light. This attracts small insects that the glowworms catch and eat.

Underwater Darkness

The deepest parts of the oceans are dark all the time. Many underwater caves are completely dark, too.

Many creatures that live in this darkness are blind. They find their way around rocks and other obstacles by "feeling" slight changes in water pressure.

Cave-dwelling fish have no eyes.

Angler fish produce tiny amounts of light to attract their food.

In the Garden

Some garden creatures are active at night.

Snails usually hide in dark, damp places during the day so that they won't dry out. They come out at night or after rain to eat plants.

Many insects are active after the sun goes down. Garden spiders mend their webs each evening so that they will be ready to catch insects during the night.

Catching a Glimpse

Some zoos have special areas for displaying nocturnal animals. These areas have bright lights on at night, so that the nocturnal animals go to sleep. Then, during the day, the displays are lit with very dim light; the animals think that it is night and become active.

These pictures were taken at night using *infrared* film.

Scientists use a special kind of light, called *infrared* light, for watching nocturnal animals. We can't see infrared light, but it can be used to produce pictures that we *can* see.

GLOSSARY

echoes - sounds that bounce off objects and travel back to where they came from

echolocation - a process of using echoes to locate objects

infrared light - a kind of light that is invisible to humans. Infrared light is given off by living things and can be used to produce pictures in the dark.

nocturnal animals - animals that are active during the night and sleep during the day

pupil - part of the eye that lets in light

tapetum - a kind of mirror inside the eyes of some nocturnal animals. The tapetum reflects light, helping the animal to see when there is little light.

INDEX

burrows 16-17
caves 2, 17, 18
deserts 14-15
echoes 10
echolocation 10
eyes 4-5, 6-7
hearing 8-9

infrared light 23
light 4, 6-7, 17, 19
oceans 2, 18-19
pupil 7
tapetum 6
zoos 22